Nocturne on LORD, I NEED YOU

MUSIC BY
Christy Nockels, Daniel Carson, Jesse Reeves, Kristian Stanfill, Matt Maher

ARRANGED FOR SOLO PIANO BY
Timothy Shaw

worship BRIDGES

NOCTURNE ON "LORD, I NEED YOU"

Music by Jesse Reeves, Kristian Stanfill, Matt Maher,
Christy Nockels and Daniel Carson
Arranged by TIMOTHY SHAW

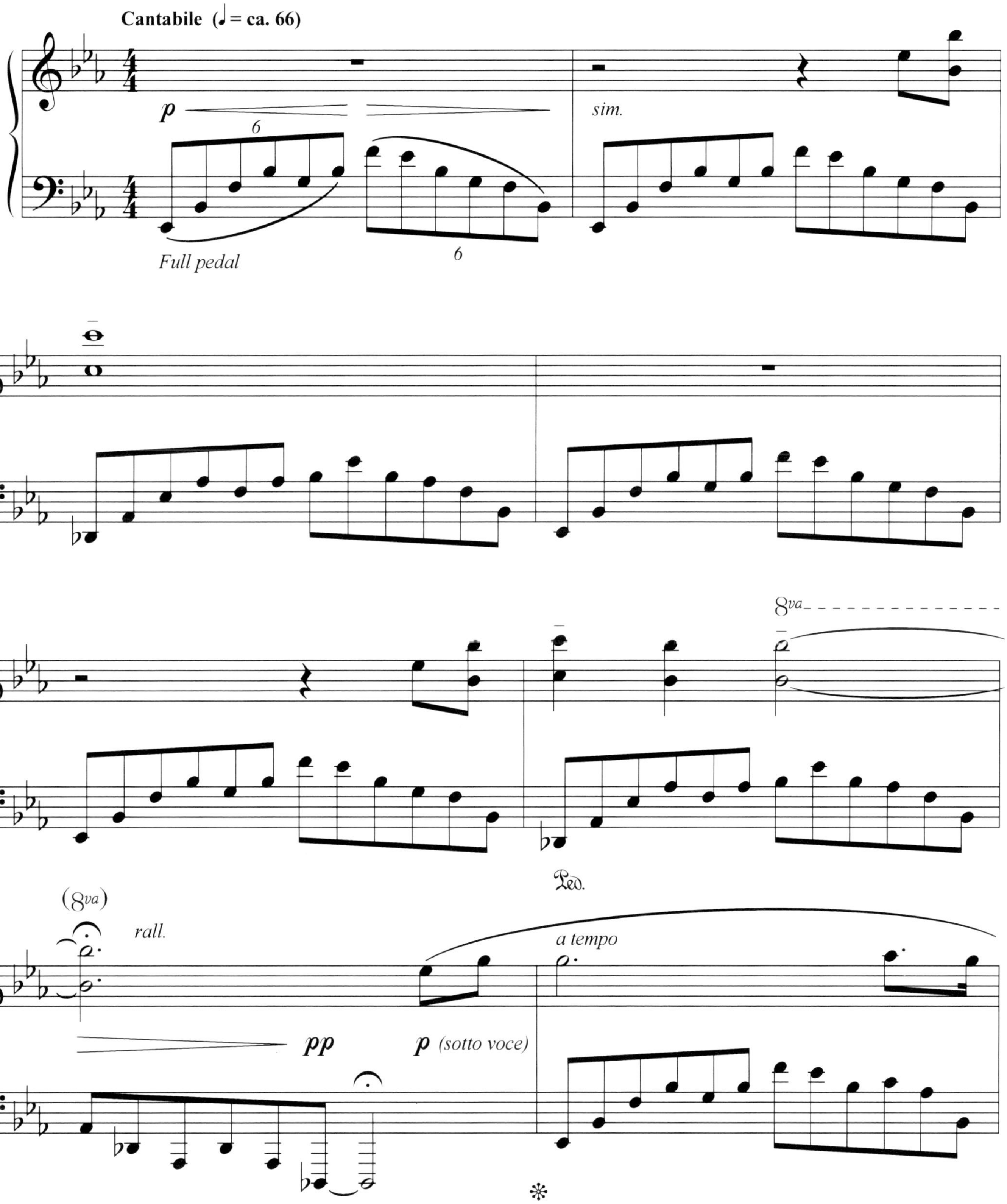

9
11
8va
13
15
rall.
17
a tempo

19
21
tr
tr
23
25
espressivo
rall.
27
a tempo
p
mp

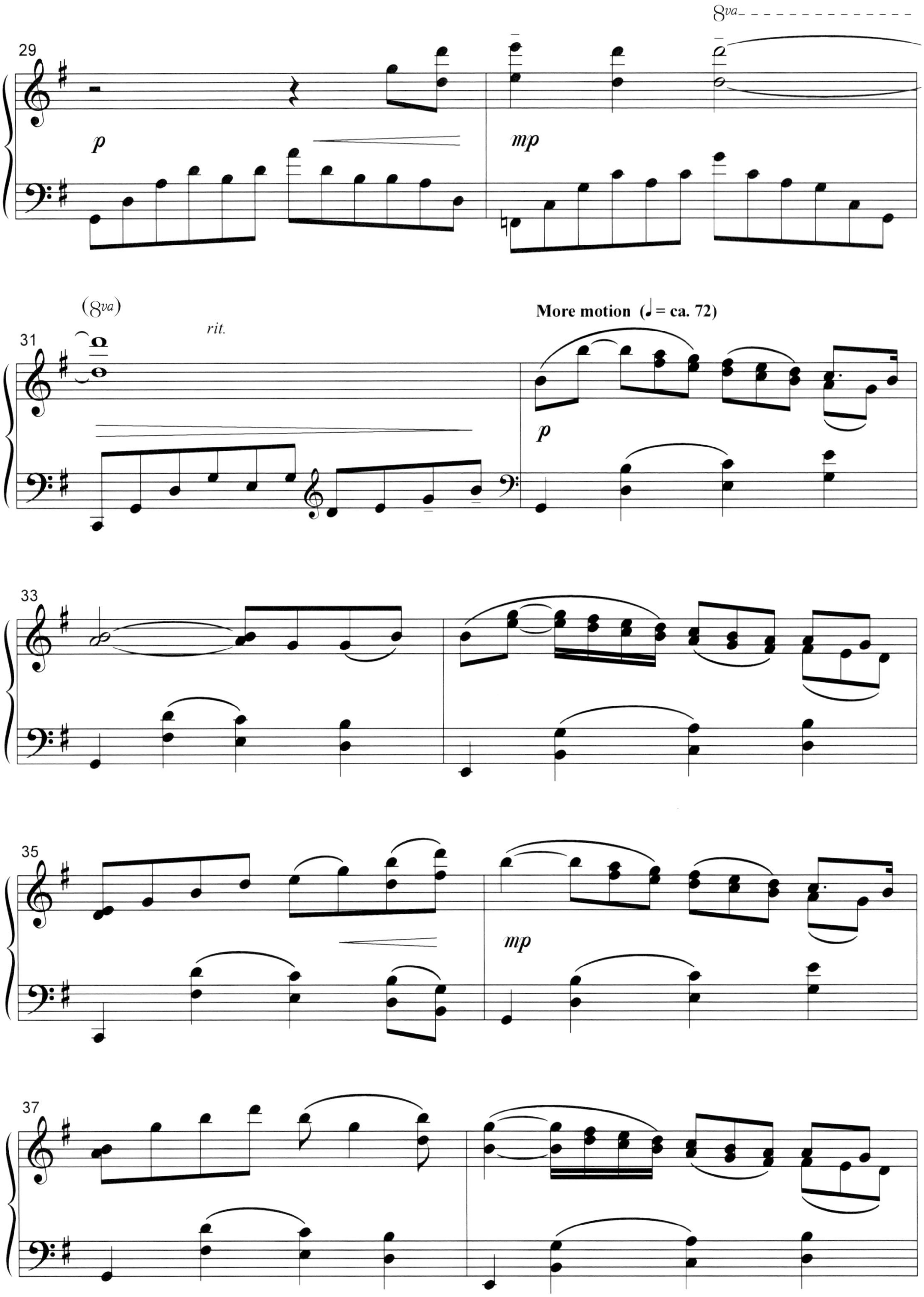
8va
29
p
mp
(8va)
rit.
31
More motion (♩ = ca. 72)
p
33
35
mp
37

mf
rall.
8va
Tempo I
f
mp
Ped.
tr

rall.
a tempo
p
8vb
8vb

63
mp
8vb
65
(ad lib) 6
13
rall.
mf
67
Ped.
Ped
69
a tempo
p
sim.
71

73
8va
rall.
pp
p (sotto voce)
Ped.
75
a tempo
6
9
77
79
tr
tr
81

stringendo
Ped.
rall.
a tempo
p
pp
delicatiss.
molto rit.
a tempo
Ped.
pp

worship

BRIDGES